30 Days
of Encouraging
Your Husband

JOURNAL

I'm so glad for your desire to build your home (Prov. 14:1) by building up and encouraging your husband! I'm confident you will experience rich spiritual growth in your own life as you seek to reflect the heart of Christ in your marriage.

Hardly a week goes by that I don't hear from women who are taking what we have called the 30-Day Husband Encouragement Challenge. Here's how it works—it has a negative side and a positive side:

- For the next 30 days, purpose not to say anything negative about your husband—not to him and not to anyone else about him.

- Every day for the next 30 days, tell your husband something that you admire or appreciate about him, something you're grateful for. And—tell someone else what you appreciate about him, as well!

Over the years, countless women have shared how God has used this simple challenge to breathe new life into their marriage. Here's just one example from a woman in Texas:

> I'm on day ten of the 30-Day Husband Encouragement Challenge. It's going great so far, and I know it will only get better from here.
>
> My husband and I have only been married three and a half years. We have a good marriage, but I decided to take this challenge because I know I struggle with

the things a lot of women struggle with. Sometimes (too often) he asks me not to treat him like a child. Or I find myself nagging about something I know I should commit to the Lord in prayer.

I've found in the first ten days of the challenge, there has been a peace that the Lord has poured on our marriage and a peace that is in my heart toward my husband. He even surprised me with a dozen roses on the evening of day eight! Thank you, *Revive Our Hearts*, for the challenge to become a better wife and servant of the Lord.

Now, I can't promise that if you take the 30-Day Husband Encouragement Challenge, your husband will send you flowers on day eight! But I do believe God will use your encouragement to challenge your husband to become more of the man and the husband that he was created to be.

This resource is designed to help you track your journey over the next 30 days. We've included some journal questions to guide you, but don't feel bound by them. More than anything, these pages are intended to be a record of what God does in your heart and in your marriage as you take this opportunity to bless your husband.

I'd also encourage you to find a friend to join you in this challenge. There will likely be days when you'll be discouraged and want to give up. Having a friend to walk with you will be so helpful.

May the Lord bless you as you seek to be an encouragement to your husband!

Nancy Leigh DeMoss

Day 1

The heart of her husband trusts in her, and he will have no lack of gain.
She does him good, and not harm, all the days of her life.
—Proverbs 31:11–12

To refresh your memory, here's the 30-Day Encouragement Challenge:

- **You can't say anything negative about your husband—to your husband . . . or to anyone else.**

- **Say something that you admire or appreciate about your husband—to your husband . . . and to someone else!**

To help you get started, have you ever thanked your husband for choosing you above all other women? He found you attractive as a person and appreciated you. Though many circumstances in your marriage may have changed, let your husband know that you are glad God led you together and that you want to be a blessing to him for the rest of your marriage. Let him know that he can trust you to be in his corner.

One of the best opportunities to express your gratitude is first thing in the morning. How do you greet your husband each morning? Is he confident in your love? Give him a wake-up call that he'll never forget—a big "I love you" and an "I'm so glad I'm your wife!"

> **"**I sort of had the feeling that my husband might get tired of me being thankful verbally every day. . . . Really, I never get tired of feeling loved and cherished by my sweetheart, so I should never stop thanking him and being grateful to him for all he does. I should never stop showing respect in a way that he can feel that it is respect. **"** —Kate

ournaling
Thought

*Write down
some reasons
you are thankful
for your
husband.*

Day 2

Through love serve one another. —Galatians 5:13

How did you do yesterday with your first day of blessing and encouraging your husband? Was it easy? Was it hard to hold your tongue when you wanted to say something negative? We hope you're off to a good start. (If you blew it, don't give up—start again today!) There are so many practical things you can praise, if you look for them.

Today, find some way that your husband is serving you or your family. Does he help around the house? Take care of the car? Fix things that are broken? If your budget allows, give him a new, small tool with a big bow attached. But make sure he doesn't think it's part of a "Honey Do" list!

Maybe your husband's not a handyman, but does he run errands for you? Let you go first? Take care of you when you are sick? Help you make decisions? Praise him for his willingness to serve others. Let him know that you see his unique service as a great strength.

> **"** *I never realized how much my husband does for our family and how wonderful of a man he can be when all I am doing is being in his corner . . . cheering for him.* **"** —Kim

Day 3

Love is patient and kind. —1 Corinthians 13:4

And my God will supply every need of yours according to his riches in glory in Christ Jesus. —Philippians 4:19

Love indeed suffers long and is kind. As you consider your Encouragement Challenge, determine today that you will not say anything negative to or about your husband. Speak kindly to him with words of genuine encouragement.

If your husband is considerate of your needs, let him know that you have noticed. Thank him for his kindness and consideration. Thank the Lord that your husband knows how to be both tough and tender.

Sometimes it's difficult for a man to be gentle, kind, or tender—especially if he hasn't had role models in these areas. If he's not a considerate person, appeal to him for help without complaining. Let him know that it's hard for you to handle some things alone. Then, when he moves in to help, don't insist that he do it your way. Be glad that he is responding, and express your gratitude.

Ultimately, you can't expect your husband to make you feel more secure, loved, etc. Remember that only God can meet the deepest needs of your heart.

Love bears all things, believes all things, hopes all things, endures all things. —1 Corinthians 13:7

Journaling Thought

How can you make it a habit to assume the best of your husband before making assumptions?

Day 4

Let him labor, doing honest work with his own hands.
—Ephesians 4:28

We are all accountable for the things we say, both negative and positive words. Have you embraced the challenge to speak only positive things to your husband and to others about him? Here's a suggestion that touches the core of your husband's world.

Some women take their husband's career for granted, and they show it in many ways. Do you "dump" on your husband at the end of the workday, or do you strengthen and encourage him with your words? A wise wife will make her husband feel that she values and appreciates his work. Let him know that you are glad he is a hard worker. Take opportunities to praise his diligence and resourcefulness to others.

If your husband is out of work, unable to work, or refuses to work, you'll need to be more creative. Praise him for a character quality that you see in him that would be a vital part of a successful career—such as persistence, decisiveness, strength, an analytical mind, organizational skills, good with people, good listener, determination, etc.

*66 The challenge has helped me to appreciate my husband
even more than I already do. I feel myself growing spiritually
and feel as if God is smiling each day. 99 —Susan*

Journaling Thought

In what areas do you need to verbally affirm your husband more often?

Day 5

Let no corrupting talk come out of your mouths, but only such as is good for building up, as fits the occasion, that it may give grace to those who hear. —Ephesians 4:29

Another way to describe the positive side of this 30-Day Encouragement Challenge is by using the word "edify," which means, "to build up." Negative comments only discourage and tear down. Positive comments encourage and build.

Do you edify your husband before others, adding to his value in their eyes? This is especially important to other family members.

Do you praise your husband to his relatives and yours? Does your husband's mother know how much you love him? How about your dad? Perhaps you can drop a word of praise into a conversation or letter. Be creative in letting your relatives know that you respect your husband, love him, and support him—in spite of whatever flaws and weaknesses he may have.

Let your speech always be gracious. —Colossians 4:6

Day 6

Whatever you do, do all to the glory of God. —1 Corinthians 10:31

Do you recognize and appreciate your husband's creativity? Or do you criticize and demean his efforts? Instead of negativity, determine to be positive. Perhaps you can help your husband see that his efforts are an opportunity to glorify God.

Is your husband the creative type? Does he have any artistic gifts? What is that special knack he has? Affirm him for his handiwork—a hobby, music, gardening, tinkering with cars, working with wood, etc. Remember, even if he doesn't measure up to your standards, praise his efforts. If your budget allows, buy him a book or magazine that will continue to encourage his special skill or talent.

If you have a hard time finding his creative side, understand that men's creativity sometimes is related to their work. Find something he does to make his job run more smoothly or something he does that adds value to his work . . . and let him know that you have noticed.

Make his day . . . praise his accomplishments in public, while he is listening.

Journaling Thought

*In what ways
is your husband
creative?
How can you
encourage
his creative
tendencies?*

Day 7

*Do not toil to acquire wealth; be discerning enough to desist.
When your eyes light on it, it is gone, for suddenly it sprouts wings,
flying like an eagle toward heaven. —Proverbs 23:4-5*

Money is the root of much marital discord. Ask yourself, *Am I being negative toward my husband in the area of finances?* Determine not to speak evil of your husband in this area. Discover ways to encourage and help him instead.

Does your husband handle finances wisely? Does he make good financial investments based on biblical principles? Does he have a budget? Does he make wise decisions about purchases—checking many sources before he buys? Is he a good steward of his money before the Lord? Let him know how much you appreciate his strengths in financial matters.

If he is weak in this area, encourage any good decisions that he does make. Perhaps you can help him, if he's open to the idea, by organizing financial files or providing other practical assistance. Or if he wants you to handle the finances, ask for his input before you make decisions that will affect him.

*An excellent wife who can find? She is far more precious than
jewels. . . . She looks well to the ways of her household and
does not eat the bread of idleness. —Proverbs 31:10, 27*

Journaling Thought

Do you support or hinder your family's financial stability? How can you encourage your husband in this area?

Day 8

But a faithful man who can find? —Proverbs 20:6

Faithfulness is a wonderful but rare quality today, especially in regard to marriage. Do you understand how important this quality is? Your challenge is to continue to root out all negative speaking, and plant seeds of encouragement instead. You may be amazed at what will grow.

Contemporary culture often entices men to be unfaithful to their wedding vows and spiritual commitments. Appreciate your husband's faithfulness—how he is loyal to you. Let him know that you are glad he has "stick-to-it-iveness" in your marriage. Appreciate his faithfulness to God.

If you have an unfaithful husband, this is undoubtedly a difficult area for you. Pray, speak the truth in love, remain faithful yourself, and discover ways to encourage faithfulness in your mate. The Bible says that husbands may be won "by the conduct of their wives" (1 Pet. 3:1). You may also want to seek counsel from a mature, godly individual or couple.

> **"**I am on day eight of the Husband Encouragement Challenge, and I never thought in a million years that such simple words could have such a profound effect on my relationship. Most importantly, I didn't realize how little I was actually praising my husband. **"** —Carolyn

Journaling Thought

Recount the ways your husband is faithful to you—big and small.

Day 9

Be quick to hear, slow to speak. —James 1:19

We are often so busy speaking that we don't take time to listen. We are so quick to offer a comment—negative or positive—that we don't really "hear" our husband's heart. Remember, we have two ears and only one mouth. We need to listen more!

As you continue in your 30-Day Challenge, not speaking negatively and focusing on positive encouragement, hear the Lord's admonition today: "Be quick to hear."

If listening is a real problem for you, play a game with yourself. See if you can listen to your husband for one whole day, only speaking when asked a question. If your husband notices the difference, explain that you are learning to listen more—not only to God, but also to him.

One easy way to express admiration for your husband is to ask a question about something he enjoys, and then listen to his response. If it's an area of personal familiarity, keep asking questions until you learn something you didn't know, then tell him, "Wow, I didn't know that!"

Make listening to your husband a priority today—even if you have to put it in your schedule!

Journaling Thought

List some questions you can ask your husband today.

Day 10

Behold, you are beautiful, my beloved, truly delightful.
—Song of Solomon 1:16

We all crave appreciation. We want to know that we are valued and loved. Early love letters probably reflected our admiration, but if we're not careful, our spouse will forget why we were drawn to him. If you still have any of your old love letters, re-read them for clues to deepen your current level of appreciation for your spouse.

When we spend time criticizing our husbands, we lose time that could be spent admiring them. As you consider various ways to encourage your husband, ask, *How can I admire him?*

Does your husband know that you think he is attractive? What was one of the characteristics in your husband that first drew you to him? Was it a physical characteristic or something else?

Was it his gentle, compassionate eyes? Kindness or concern for others? An easygoing confidence? A steadiness that comes from trusting in the Lord? Strength of character in a culture that lacks integrity? Do you see at least a glimpse of that characteristic in him today? Whatever it is, tell him!

"*I began your 30 days of encouragement for your husband. It has helped me to think of things that I had forgotten I loved about this man! I am so grateful that this was suggested to me. God is really working in all our lives!* **"** —Debbie

journal

Day 11

Wives, submit to your own husbands, as to the Lord. —Ephesians 5:22

Women who are constantly negative toward their husbands—especially by speaking evil of them to others—show great disrespect. Determine not to do that today (or ever!). This challenge to encourage is closely connected to submission.

Men respond to women who respect them. What do you respect about your husband? Part of that respect includes submission to his authority. Let your husband know how respecting him makes it easier to submit to his leadership. Show your respect in public by listening to him and smiling at him when he speaks. Place your hand in his as you walk together.

If you feel there is nothing to respect, search harder . . . nearly every man has some core characteristic that can be nurtured and respected. In any case, you must still cultivate a submissive spirit to his position of leadership "as to the Lord."

Therefore be imitators of God, as beloved children. And walk in love, as Christ loved us and gave himself up for us, a fragrant offering and sacrifice to God. —Ephesians 5:1-2

Journaling Thought

*How is
your husband
respectable?*

Day 12

With all humility and gentleness, with patience,
bearing with one another in love. —Ephesians 4:2

Part of the difficulty you may face as you continue in this 30-Day Challenge to encourage your husband is that you really are struggling to find positive things to praise. Perhaps the problem is not with your husband. Have you checked your own heart?

Sometimes we get disillusioned because of our own unreasonable or unrealistic expectations (Prov. 13:12). It may not be that our mates are doing something wrong; it's simply that we expect too much in some areas.

Our expectations must be met in God alone, and then we will have the right perspective to ask God for the healing and grace we need to respond to others.

How sad that we give more grace to others than to those in our own homes. Today, try to look at your husband through eyes of grace. Verbally thank your husband for what he is already doing.

❝*Through praying for my husband, God had changed my mind, my outlook, and my perspective. Glory to God! He has renewed the right spirit in me, and I am so thankful.***❞** —Paula

Journaling Thought

Describe ways God has shown grace to you. Examine ways you can extend that same grace to your husband.

Day 13

I am my beloved's, and his desire is for me. —Song of Solomon 7:10

The sexual relationship. It's one of those elements—along with money and children—that can derail a marriage through negative comments. Negativity destroys intimacy, but encouragement builds and strengthens the marriage bond.

Let's get practical here. Is your husband a good lover? Have you told him so? Be specific. Let him know when he pleases you. Most husbands genuinely want to please their wives, especially in this important area of marriage.

In moments of intimacy, do you find your mind wandering? This can change as you focus on something wonderful about your husband. Realize that your husband wants intimacy with you . . . his desire is toward you.

Does this area of your marriage need some work? Remember that this is a sensitive area for men. Be sure to encourage his lovemaking and masculinity in positive ways.

"I was in disbelief about this challenge, but I did it anyway. My willingness and God's perfect will brought back the wonderful love and romance He intends for every marriage. Thanks!" —Valerie

Journaling Thought

Does your husband feel affirmed by you romantically?

Day 14

The righteous who walks in his integrity—
blessed are his children after him! —Proverbs 20:7

Every week there are news reports about men who gave in to temptations and compromised what they said they believed. We hear countless reports about dishonest business dealings, hidden infidelity, and hypocritical leaders. It's so easy to focus on these things and ignore those who are being honest, faithful, and genuine. As you continue in the 30-Day Encouragement Challenge, determine to look for ways that your husband stands against the culture.

Is your spouse a man of integrity? Is he fair in his dealings with people? Does he understand the meaning of justice? Is he honest in business? Un-hypocritical in his faith? Consider all the ways a man can live in integrity, and praise your husband for one of them.

As you have the opportunity—as it is appropriate—share examples of your husband's honesty and integrity with others.

I therefore . . . urge you to walk in a manner
worthy of the calling to which you have been called,
with all humility and gentleness, with patience,
bearing with one another in love, eager to maintain
the unity of the Spirit in the bond of peace.
—Ephesians 4:1–3

RECOGNIZE SPIRITUAL GROWTH

Day 15

*Grow in the grace and knowledge of our Lord
and Savior Jesus Christ.* —2 Peter 3:18

Sometimes we live so close to our spouse that we fail to see him as others do; we only see our husband's faults. But take a step back. Perhaps he is growing spiritually in ways you have failed to appreciate. How can you encourage his growth in a fresh, new way? Remember, your husband is accountable to God for his spiritual development. You are accountable to God to encourage and not hinder that growth.

Can you identify an area of spiritual strength in your husband? Does he pray or read his Bible regularly? Does he like to read about or discuss spiritual matters? Does he go to church with you? Is he a spiritual leader? What do others say about him? If you can identify a specific area, praise him for that.

If not, pray earnestly that God will work in his heart, and watch for signs of spiritual growth in the future.

❝Well, I'm the one who was surprised, because it was like everything I was supposed to be doing in this challenge, my husband was doing and excelling at it better than me! I can't be encouraging in my own strength, and I need Him to daily help me to love my wonderful hubby as he truly deserves.❞ —Mercy

Journaling Thought

How can you encourage your husband's spiritual growth (without nagging)? Don't forget to examine your own heart and spiritual growth as well.

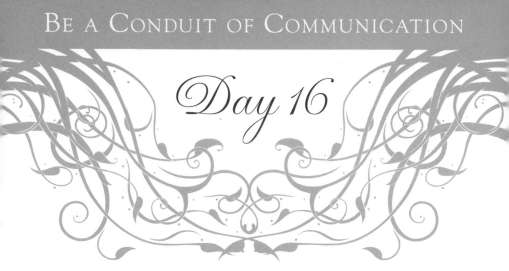

Day 16

Then the LORD God said, "It is not good that the man should be alone; I will make him a helper fit for him." —Genesis 2:18

God says that it is not good for man to be alone—but the way some women criticize their mates, the husbands may long for solitude. Be careful today not to criticize your mate, but look instead for ways to encourage him personally and publicly.

Speaking of communication, does your husband communicate with you? God has made you a companion and helper for your husband, and part of being "one flesh" with him is the privilege of sharing and discussing personal needs and concerns. Thank God for that wonderful gift. Thank your husband for communicating with you.

If your spouse does not communicate as you wish, look for ways that he communicates that are normal for him: smiling at you, nodding his head—even a pleasant grunt—and then thank him for letting you know that he cares. Perhaps he needs to be lovingly taught how to communicate. Be patient with him . . . and listen when he does speak.

> **"**My husband—the hard-hearted, closed-off, non-communicative husband—broke down, opened up, listened instead of barking orders, and sat on the couch with me last night. He said, 'This is the best week I've ever had! To just be here holding my wife in my arms is the best way to end a day!' **"** —Stephanie

Day 17

*She opens her mouth with wisdom, and the
teaching of kindness is on her tongue. —Proverbs 31:26*

Are you a wise woman? Do you open your mouth with wisdom, as Proverbs
31:26 suggests? As you continue in this 30-Day Challenge, remember
that a wise woman encourages her husband.

Is your husband a wise man? Does he have a godly perspective that
comes from knowing God and walking with Him in obedience? Does he
have a sense of purpose for his life and vision for your home? Tell him
how much this means to you.

If you are not sure about your husband's vision for your home, ask him,
"Honey, what do you want to accomplish with our marriage and home
in the years to come?" and "How can I help you accomplish that?" If he
does not have a vision, your questions may inspire him to develop one.

If your husband is not walking with God—or perhaps, does not know
the Lord—you have the opportunity and responsibility to practice your
faith and create a thirst for God. Thank God for giving your husband
a place in his heart that only He can fill, and keep praying that he will
turn to the Lord to fill that vacuum!

*The fear of the LORD is the beginning of wisdom, and the
knowledge of the Holy One is insight. —Proverbs 9:10*

journal

Day 18

You make known to me the path of life; in your presence there is fullness of joy. . . . Blessed are the people whose God is the LORD!
—Psalm 16:11; 144:15

A joyful heart is good medicine. —Proverbs 17:22

It's hard to criticize others when we are enjoying their company. Instead of speaking negatively to your husband today, enjoy him! Encourage him! As you experience fullness of joy with God, share some of that joy with your husband.

Does your husband have a playful side? A great sense of humor? Is there a "little boy" who wants to escape from time to time, reflecting the joy in his heart?

This is a wonderful part of who he is and a great strength. Let him know that you appreciate his joyfulness and his playful spirit. Find opportunities to join him in positive playtimes.

If your husband can sometimes be overly serious, coax him out occasionally for some playtimes. It will help him relieve stress and relax.

> **❝**I am not naturally a gift giver; however, gift giving is one of my husband's first love languages. On the way home . . . I felt like the Lord gave me the thought to go in and get my husband his favorite drink. Immediately, I was delighted by the idea of surprising him with this small gift. **❞** —Kristy

Journaling Thought

What "positive playtime" can you join your husband in today? Be spontaneous!

Day 19

Read a wife's description of her beloved in Song of Solomon 5:10–16.

Criticism leaves scars, but encouragement can bring healing. Remember that today as you focus on your 30-Day Encouragement Challenge.

Almost nothing is as devastating to a man as the belief that his wife finds him repulsive. Sadly, many women unwisely criticize their husbands' bodies.

Have you ever considered how wonderfully God designed men and women? No matter how a man looks—by the standards of the world—a loving God designed them all, and they are all beautiful in His sight. Encourage your husband today by praising his uniqueness.

As you look over your husband's body, from the tip of his toes to his bald or bushy head, thank God that your husband is "wonderfully made," then admire your husband verbally. (Strong arms? Hairy chest? Firm hands? Big feet? Rugged chin? Wide shoulders? Compassionate eyes? Broad smile?)

My beloved is radiant and ruddy, distinguished
among ten thousand. —Song of Solomon 5:10

Journaling Thought

Describe the physical characteristics you admire in your husband. Be sure to tell him today what those things are.

Day 20

*Be kind to one another, tenderhearted, forgiving one another,
as God in Christ forgave you.* —Ephesians 4:32

It's time for some heart examination. As you continue in this 30-Day Challenge, have you found any roots of bitterness that are contaminating your relationship with your husband? Do you understand that as long as you are unwilling to forgive your husband—by God's grace and in His power—you will not be able to encourage him? Your own resentment will keep getting in the way. Now is the time to deal with any unforgiving attitudes. Forgive him, even as God has forgiven you.

Is your husband a forgiving man? Does he keep short accounts of your problems? Express your thankfulness for such a man.

Does your husband—rightly or wrongly—harbor grudges against you? Again, are there things you need to change, or do you need to ask for his forgiveness for an offense? Help your husband be more forgiving by quickly forgiving him for his mistakes.

*"You're never more like Jesus, you're never more like God,
than when you are forgiving and pursuing reconciliation."*
—Nancy Leigh DeMoss

journal

Day 21

But seek first the kingdom of God and His righteousness, and all these things will be added to you. —Matthew 6:33

If we are living in light of eternity, everything we think, do, or say is seen from an eternal perspective. We will someday give an account for our failure to speak words of love and encouragement. Determine today that your words will be sweet and helpful.

Does your husband have an eternal perspective that allows him to reject materialism and temporal values? Express your gratefulness for his value system, and praise him for putting eternal things before riches and other things of this world.

If this is a problem area for him, consider how you might alter your own value system and live for eternity in front of him, encouraging him to do the same. Only two things will go into eternity . . . the Word of God and people. Be sure that you are focusing on the right things today.

> **"**I just completed the 30-Day Husband Encouragement Challenge. I can see that my kindness and encouragement to my husband has softened his heart. The other day, he told me that we need to start praying together for a particular neighbor. This was encouraging to me that he saw his leadership in the home. **"** —Julia

journal

Day 22

*Set your minds on things that are above,
not on things that are on earth.* —Colossians 3:2

Focus today on how you represent your husband in your home, your church, and your community. In this challenge to encourage, ask yourself: *If all my family and friends knew about my husband came from a filter of what I've said about him, what would they think of my husband?* Do you need to change the filter?

Do you talk positively about your husband to others . . . or do you complain and criticize? Your speech should reflect 1 Corinthians 13 love. Your words should be kind and should never "rejoice at wrongdoing" (v. 6). Refrain from listing your husband's faults to others. Satan likes to trick us in this area. Be wary of sharing barbed "prayer requests."

Remember, "love covers a multitude of sins" (1 Pet. 4:8). Present your husband before others today in a strong, positive manner. Slip in a good word for your spouse. Resist the urge to correct or belittle him in front of others. Some of what you say may come back to him—and you want your words to be sweet—building him up and never tearing him down.

Don't forget, you are always criticizing—or encouraging—before an audience. God hears your conversations when you are alone with your husband in your own home. May your speech be always seasoned with grace.

journal

Day 23

Let your speech always be gracious. —Colossians 4:6

Show yourself in all respects to be a model of good works. —Titus 2:7

Does the 30-Day Encouragement Challenge seem like hard work? Or is it becoming a pleasant exercise in genuine Christ-likeness within your home? You are only scratching the surface of ways to encourage your mate.

Is your husband organized? Is he diligent? Is he persistent? These are all related to a pattern of personal disciplines that are worthy of your praise. Affirm him for one or more of these traits that you see in him.

Some men have not developed these qualities because they are naturally more spontaneous. You can praise his spontaneity! Perhaps God has called you alongside to help him with disciplines he has not yet developed—but this does not include nagging. You can keep him organized.

Whatever the need, you can be your husband's cheerleader, encouraging him when he wants to give up.

> **"**I went to my husband with my concerns without nagging or complaining, and I humbled myself (which was a challenge) and said, 'I need your help, because I can't do it alone.' That very second, my husband hugged me and grabbed the vacuum and got to work. Thank you so much for your program!**"** —Amy

Journaling Thought

Are you living a lifestyle that would naturally encourage discipline in your husband?

Day 24

Fathers, do not provoke your children to anger, but bring them up in the discipline and instruction of the Lord. —Ephesians 6:4

Children can be quite a challenge to the marriage relationship. A wise wife will support her husband's leadership in the home as much as possible and will praise him for his fathering skills. Negativity makes a man feel like a failure and may make him want to give up.

Does your husband discipline your children wisely? Does he show them love and encourage them? Does he take an interest in their activities and dreams? Does he spend time with them? Does he take part in developing their character? Praise him for these important life skills.

If you don't have children, is your husband positive and encouraging around other people's children? Let him know that you have noticed.

If your husband does not experience positive relationships with children, you will need to figure out why. Perhaps he had negative experiences as a child with his own parents and needs to learn how to respond. Perhaps you can lovingly and patiently show him how to parent—while still maintaining his authority in the home.

❝My husband used to have so much stress from work and being a father of eight that he would take it out on us. As I learned something new each day to say or do for him to make him feel better and more appreciated for the things he does, he began to soften. I picture him softening under the hand of God.❞ —Shanna

journal

Day 25

Seek peace and pursue it. —Psalm 34:14

*You keep him in perfect peace whose mind is stayed on you,
because he trusts in you.* —Isaiah 26:3

Before you consider whether these verses describe your husband, consider your own presence in the home. Do you promote an atmosphere of peace, or do critical words often flow from your mouth? Do you struggle with anger? If so, before you continue with your Encouragement Challenge, confess these sinful habits to the Lord, and determine to speak words of peace to your family today.

Does your husband bring an atmosphere of peace into your home? Is his presence a calming influence? Does he bring music, entertainment, books, or people into your home that build a sense of serenity? Let him know how much you appreciate this wonderful quality, and support his choices.

If, on the other hand, he is quickly angered or he creates chaos rather than calm, ask God to give you an abundance of the kind of peace that will speak to his heart. Be patient and loving. Create an inviting atmosphere of peace, as much as possible.

*And let the peace of Christ rule in your hearts, to which
indeed you were called in one body. And be thankful.*
—Colossians 3:15

Journaling
Thought

What can you do to promote a lifetime environment of peace in your home?

Day 26

And Jesus increased in wisdom and in stature
and in favor with God and men. —Luke 2:52

If you have faithfully encouraged your husband, you will no doubt have seen some changes in his life . . . and your own life, as well. Encouragement is a wonderful habit that we hope you will continue for the rest of your life.

The important thing is to keep growing in Christ and obeying the Word of God as you respond to your husband. As you consider today how to bless your husband and not tear him down, think of ways that you can encourage balance in your home.

Jesus led a balanced life. He grew mentally, physically, spiritually, and socially. As you see your husband branching out in these areas, is there a pattern of growth? Is your husband striving for balance in his life? If so, let him know you have noticed, and ask how you can further encourage that balance.

If your husband is out of balance—focusing on one area to the exclusion of the others—consider whether there are things you can do to help restore or create balance in his life. Can you encourage times for sports or exercise? Keep the children quiet for a study time? Invite friends over for dinner? Stimulate his mind?

Be sure you are working toward balance in your own life, as well. Be an example!

Day 27

Be strong, and let your heart take courage,
all you who wait for the LORD! —Psalm 31:24

You have almost completed the 30-Day Husband Encouragement Challenge. Perhaps it has taken you a tremendous amount of courage to speak words of encouragement consistently to your husband. Courage comes as we place our trust in God. Have faith that God will continue to work long after your encouraging words have been shared.

There are lots of "tough guys" in the world, but true courage comes from the Lord. Does your husband exhibit the courage to take an unpopular stand, perhaps even to stand alone against evil? Is he courageous in his faith? Does he work hard to change injustice? Is he a stickler for the truth? Does he protect you or your family from the attacks of the Enemy?

Psalm 27:14 says this kind of courage comes from "waiting" on the Lord for His strength. If your budget allows, "award" your husband with a medal, trophy, framed picture of a brave knight, or some other token that represents his courage as a man of God. Praise evidences of your husband's courage in protecting you, your marriage, your family, or your home.

> **"**I started the 30-Day Husband Encouragement Challenge just two days before my husband was laid off from his job. It was such a blessing to receive ideas for encouraging him and lifting him up during that time. **"** —Ginny

Day 28

*The fear of the LORD is instruction in wisdom,
and humility comes before honor.* —Proverbs 15:33

Sometimes, when we just "know" we are right and our husbands are wrong, it takes great humility to honor them. It is difficult to speak well of our husbands when our own hearts are puffed up with pride.

As part of your Encouragement Challenge today, pray that you will respond to the Lord in faith and humility before you react to your husband. Speak wisely and well, and leave the results to God.

The humility that comes from a right relationship with God—the humility that comes when a man is willing to listen to God and be taught from His Word—is indeed a beautiful quality. Jesus was an example of this kind of humility when he was willing to submit to His Father's will (Matt. 26:39; John 6:38).

Does your husband have that kind of humility? Is he willing to learn from and submit to direction from the Lord? Let your husband know how precious this is to your marriage relationship.

> **"**I just wanted to tell you how much the 30-Day Husband Encouragement Challenge has been blessing me. I found it 'by accident' online after a particularly awful and bitter argument with my husband, and I finally decided I needed God's help.**"**
> —Louise

Day 29

The prudent sees danger and hides himself,
but the simple go on and suffer for it. —Proverbs 27:12

As you near the end of your Encouragement Challenge, take time to think about your husband's responses to the wickedness of the culture, the media, etc. Does your husband recognize and avoid evil? Does he regularly turn his back on pornography, sexual temptations, and the urge to lie and cheat?

This is a valuable character trait. Like Joseph in the Old Testament, who fled from the wicked advances of Potiphar's wife, this takes an understanding that these kinds of sins are first and foremost sins against God (Gen. 39:9).

Praise your husband when he recognizes and turns his back on wickedness. If you can think of a circumstance where your husband stood for righteousness, remind him of that today—and express your gratitude.

❝Last night was the pinnacle of the experience. It was my husband's birthday, so I threw him a party, and as gifts, each guest had to give my husband a word of encouragement or affirmation. It was wonderful.❞ —Cheryl

Journaling Thought

Can you remember a specific time when your husband promoted righteousness in your home? How can you help promote a spirit of righteousness?

Journal

Day 30

This is my beloved and this is my friend. —Song of Solomon 5:16

Friends can be completely honest with each other, but friendships are strained when truth is not spoken in love. How are you speaking to your beloved? Are you so "used" to him that you don't appreciate the wonder of his friendship? That is your challenge today. Is your sweetheart your best friend? Does he know this? Have you told him, or do you assume he "just knows"?

Friendship is something that is cultivated through the good times and the bad. Friends can share their hearts, but they don't step on each other's hearts.

The way to have and be a good friend is to cultivate and celebrate the relationship. As you end this 30-Day Encouragement Challenge, celebrate your friendship with your husband. Get alone and reflect on your beloved friend. Write him a letter listing the qualities you admire and appreciate about him. If you are creative with words, maybe you could write and frame a poem about him. Perhaps you can prepare a special meal, just for the two of you, and read the letter or poem to him.

Ask if you can pray for him and, if he is willing, thank God for your love and friendship asking for His blessing on your home. Encouragement, as you have seen these past 30 days, is a synonym for love in action.

"This is my commandment, that you love one another
as I have loved you." —John 15:12

journal

Conclusion

How has this challenge changed your heart and life, dear friend? Did God encourage you as you planned ways to encourage your husband? Were there difficult days where you simply needed to trust that God was working? Days when it was hard to leave the results to God?

Remember that God is faithful, and He will bless you for your obedience to Him. His ways are not our ways and perhaps He will honor you in ways you do not expect, but one thing is sure—you will never be the same because of your commitment to be more like Christ!

What kinds of victories have you experienced in your home since you started the 30-Day Encouragement Challenge? Would you take a moment to share these victories with us?

Revive Our Hearts
PO Box 2000
Niles, MI 49120

Info@ReviveOurHearts.com

www.ReviveOurHearts.com